KIDS ON EARTH

Wildlife Adventures – Explore The World

Ibex - Israel

Sensei Paul David

COPYRIGHT PAGE

Kids On Earth: Wildlife Adventures - Explore The World

Ibex - Israel

by Sensei Paul David,

Copyright © 2023.

All rights reserved.

978-1-77848-179-6 KoE_WildLife_Amazon_PaperbackBook_israel_ibex

978-1-77848-178-9 KoE_WildLife_Amazon_eBook_israel_ibex

978-1-77848-420-9 KoE_Wildlife_Ingram_Paperbackbook_IbexGoat

This book is not authorized for free distribution copying.

www.senseipublishing.com

@senseipublishing
#senseipublishing

Synopsis

This book is all about the amazing Ibex of Israel. It provides 30 fun facts about them, from their diet to their physical characteristics. Readers will learn about their long horns, their herbivore diet, their agility and strength, their social behavior, their intelligence, and their loyalty to their herd. By the end of this book, readers will have a better understanding of this unique and fascinating animal, and will never forget the 30 fun facts they learned.

Get Our FREE Books Now!

kidsonearth.life

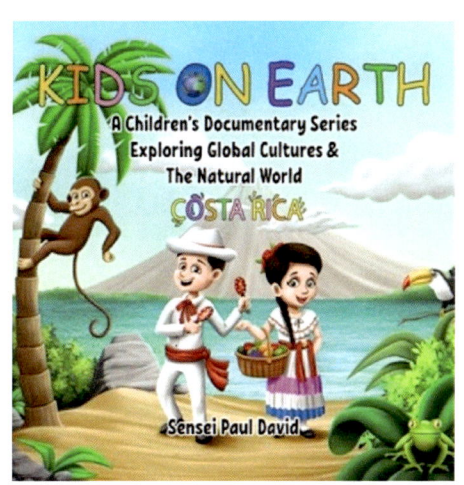

kidsonearth.world

Click Below for Another Book In Each Series

senseipublishing.com/KoE_SERIES

senseipublishing.com/KoE_Wildlife_SERIES

KoE En Español

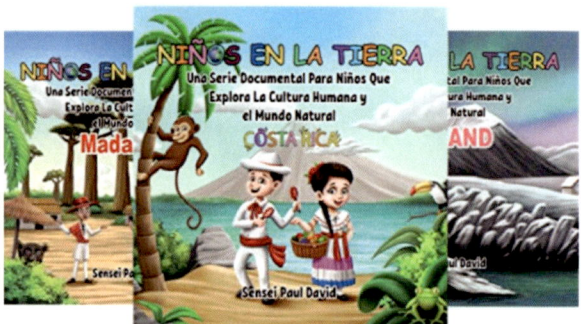

senseipublishing.com/KoE_SERIES_SPANISH

www.senseipublishing.com

Join Our Publishing Journey!

If you would like to receive FUTURE FREE BOOKS and get to know us better, please click www.senseipublishing.com and join our newsletter by entering your email address in the pop-up box.

Follow Our Blog: senseipauldavid.ca

Follow/Like/Subscribe: Facebook, Instagram, YouTube: @senseipublishing

Scan the QR Code with your phone or tablet to follow us on social media:

Like / Subscribe / Follow

Introduction

Welcome to the wonderful world of the amazing Ibex of Israel! The Ibex is a species of wild goat that can be found in the rocky mountains of Israel. They are very unique and fascinating creatures, and this book is here to share 30 fun facts about them that you'll never forget! From their diet to their physical characteristics, this book will provide you with all the information you need to know about these wonderful animals. So let's get started!

The Ibex is a medium-sized goat, with males reaching a maximum height of 3 feet and weighing up to 180 pounds.

The Ibex has a lifespan of up to 17 years in the wild.

The Ibex is a very curious animal, and can often be seen investigating its surroundings.

The Ibex is a territorial animal, and males will often mark their territory with their horns to keep other males away.

The Ibex is an excellent climber and can climb up steep rock faces with ease.

The Ibex is a herbivore, meaning it eats only plants and grasses.

The Ibex has a long, curved horn that can reach up to two feet in length!

The Ibex is a diurnal animal, meaning it is active during the daytime and sleeps at night.

The Ibex is a very vocal animal, with males producing loud, honking calls to announce their presence.

The Ibex is a very agile animal, and can jump up to 5 feet in the air!

The Ibex is a very strong animal, and can carry up to 200 pounds on its back!

The Ibex is a very fast animal, and can reach speeds of up to 40 miles per hour!

The Ibex has a thick, shaggy coat which helps to keep it warm in the cold mountain climate.

The Ibex is a very alert animal, and can sense danger from up to a mile away.

The Ibex is a very intelligent animal, and has been known to use tools to get food.

The Ibex is a very social animal, and can often be seen playing and interacting with other members of its herd.

The Ibex is a very adaptable animal, and can survive in a variety of different habitats.

The Ibex is a social creature, and can often be found in herds of up to 30 individuals.

The Ibex is a very strong swimmer, and can swim up to 20 miles in a single day!

The Ibex is a very loyal animal, and will often stay with the same herd for its entire life.

The Ibex is a very fast learner, and can quickly adapt to new environments.

The Ibex is a very brave animal, and will often stand its ground when threatened.

The Ibex is a very intelligent animal, and can often be seen using its horns to balance and maneuver in difficult terrain.

The Ibex is a very powerful animal, and can break through thick brush and undergrowth with ease.

The Ibex is a very resourceful animal, and has been known to find food in even the harshest of environments.

The Ibex is a very patient animal, and will often wait patiently for hours until it finds the right food.

The Ibex is a very strong animal, and can easily break through thick ice with its horns.

The Ibex is a very social animal, and will often form close bonds with other members of its herd.

The Ibex is a very loyal animal, and will often return to the same area every year to mate and raise its young.

The Ibex is a very active animal, and can travel up to 20 miles a day in search of food.

Conclusion

The Ibex of Israel is a truly remarkable and fascinating creature, and this book has hopefully shared some of the incredible facts about them with you. From their diet to their physical characteristics, the Ibex is a truly unique and amazing animal. And now you know 30 fun facts about them that you'll never forget.

Thank you for reading this book!

If you found this book helpful, I would be grateful if you would **post an honest review on Amazon** so this book can reach other supportive readers like you!

All you need to do is digitally flip to the back and leave your review. Or visit amazon.com/author/senseipauldavid click the correct book cover and click on the blue link next to the yellow stars that say, "customer reviews."

As always...

It's a great day to be alive!

Share Our FREE eBooks Now!

kidsonearth.life

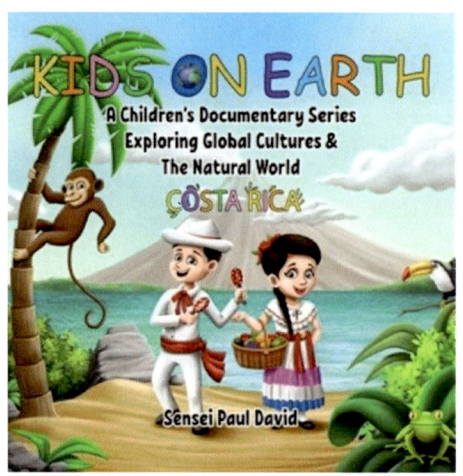

kidsonearth.world

Click Below for Another Book In Each Series

senseipublishing.com/KoE_SERIES   senseipublishing.com/KoE_Wildlife_SERIES

KoE En Español

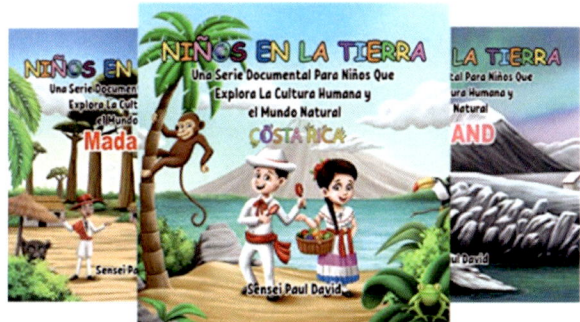

senseipublishing.com/KoE_SERIES_SPANISH

www.senseipublishing.com

www.senseipublishing.com

@senseipublishing
#senseipublishing

Check out our **recommendations** for other books for adults & kids plus other great resources by visiting
www.senseipublishing.com/resources/

Join Our Publishing Journey!

If you would like to receive FREE BOOKS and special offers, please visit www.senseipublishing.com and join our newsletter by entering your email address in the pop-up box

Follow Our Engaging Blog NOW!
senseipauldavid.ca

Get Our FREE Books Today!

Click & Share the Links Below

FREE Kids Books
lifeofbailey.senseipublishing.com
kidsonearth.senseipublishing.com

FREE Self-Development Book

senseiselfdevelopment.senseipublishing.com

FREE BONUS!!!
Experience Over 25 FREE Engaging Guided Meditations!

Prized Skills & Practices for Adults & Kids. Help Restore Deep Sleep, Lower Stress, Improve Posture, Navigate Uncertainty & More.

Download the Free Insight Timer App and click the link below:
http://insig.ht/sensei_paul

About Sensei Publishing

Sensei Publishing commits itself to helping people of all ages transform into better versions of themselves by providing high-quality and research-based self-development books with an emphasis on mental health and guided meditations. Sensei Publishing offers well-written e-books, audiobooks, paperbacks, and online courses that simplify complicated but practical topics in line with its mission to inspire people toward positive transformation.

It's a great day to be alive!

About the Author

I create simple & transformative eBooks & Guided Meditations for Adults & Children proven to help navigate uncertainty, solve niche problems & bring families closer together.

I'm a former finance project manager, private pilot, jiu-jitsu instructor, musician & former University of Toronto Fitness Trainer. I prefer a science-based approach to focus on these & other areas in my life to stay humble & hungry to evolve. I hope you enjoy my work and I'd love to hear your feedback.

- It's a great day to be alive!
Sensei Paul David

Scan & Follow/Like/Subscribe: Facebook, Instagram, YouTube: @senseipublishing

Scan using your phone/iPad camera for Social Media
Visit us at www.senseipublishing.com and sign up for our newsletter to learn more about our exciting books and to experience our FREE Guided Meditations for Kids & Adults.

www.ingramcontent.com/pod-product-compliance
Lightning Source LLC
Chambersburg PA
CBRC090902080526
44587CB00008B/165